T0101905

The

A
to
Z

of
Grandparent
Names

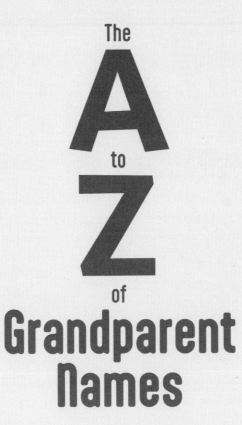

The A to Z of Grandparent Names

13-Digit ISBN: 978-1-64643-380-3
10-Digit ISBN: 1-64643-380-7

This book may be ordered by mail from the publisher. Please include $5.99 for postage and handling. Please support your local bookseller first!

Books published by Cider Mill Press Book Publishers are available at special discounts for bulk purchases in the United States by corporations, institutions, and other organizations. For more information, please contact the publisher.

Cider Mill Press Book Publishers
"Where good books are ready for press"
501 Nelson Place
Nashville, Tennessee 37214

cidermillpress.com

Printed in China

Typography: Aptly, Aria Text G2

All vectors used under official license from Shutterstock.com.

23 24 25 26 27 TYC 5 4 3 2 1
First Edition

The

A
to
Z

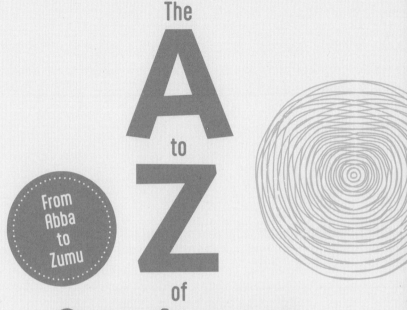

From
Abba
to
Zumu

of
Grandparent
Names

by Katie Hankinson

CIDER MILL
PRESS

BOOK
PUBLISHERS

CONTENTS

Introduction

I'm an unlikely author for this book. I'm not a grandparent, I'm not close to granting my parents grandchildren, and I have very limited experience being a granddaughter, if I'm totally honest. My grandparents' and great-grandmother's names were Margery and Albert "Hank" Hankinson, Gertrude Struble, and Helen Lewis. But to me they were Grandma Marge and Grandpa Hank, Nana Gert, and Gee. They passed away when I was young (except for Grandpa Hank, who passed when I was 18). But loving them and their loving me—it's not a love I could describe in great detail, but I remember exactly how it feels.

I remember feeling Nana holding me close to her tiny body when she came to visit us. Standing on Grandma Marge's mobility scooter as she drove us up the path to the family cabin in Pennsylvania. Talking with

Gee on her 99th birthday, knowing that she loved me even when she wasn't sure who I was. Talking with Grandpa over the phone my senior year of high school, telling him about articles I was writing in my journalism class, his asking if I could send him physical copies.

I think a lot about grandparents who have loved me who weren't technically mine. My friend Nikole's grandmother, Donna, who kindly took care of me on school trips, and who always shared a laugh with me when I visited Nikole's home. An older gentleman, Paul, whom I worked with at the adventure park in Glenwood, Colorado, who read the first chapters of my very first book (which will never see the light of day) and gasped and said, "Katie, that is beautiful. Absolutely gorgeous, gal." I think about my husband's grandmother, Gran, who upon meeting me enveloped me in a huge, floral-print hug, and said, "Welcome to the family" and "Call me Gran."

Storytelling is an important part of a family's legacy, and no one knows this better than grandparents. The names we give our grandparents are stories within themselves. When you're picking out your own grandparent honorific, it doesn't necessarily have to be something from within these pages. It can be a memory, a joke, a story, or something inspired by another name you come across (maybe in this book!).

Whether you choose a name that's popular in a familiar culture, borrow from your own grandparents, select a name that is formal or funny, or don't choose it yourself at all, at the end of the day it's simply an honor to be a grandparent. I hope this book adds to the excitement you find in your growing family and helps lead you to your grandparent name.

I understand that you may feel a resistance to being called Grandma or Grandpa. Maybe it feels older than you are or too simple compared to all the new names out there (and I assure you, there are plenty of unique options to choose from, as you'll soon learn). There are a multitude of different ways to honor grandparents from a myriad of cultural traditions, which I encourage you to delve into as you read. Consider how you use your grandparent name to call back to your roots, and take the opportunity to familiarize yourself with the ways people do this all around the world!

Grandma and Grandpa, Babushka and Dedushka, Oma and Opa—these names are near and dear to our hearts. In this book, you will uncover the origins of these names in various languages and cultures, celebrate the special bond between grandparent and grandchild, and learn something new about the world (and maybe even yourself!). You may recognize the names you called your own grandparents in these pages. With fun and unique names alongside those born out of time-honored tradition, this book is perfect for grandparents deciding what they want to be called.

In these pages, you'll find over 100 names from all over, with an in-depth look at the stories behind each of them. Whether you want to honor your ancestors or capture the relationship you have with your grandchild, find a name as special as you are in *The A to Z of Grandparent Names*.

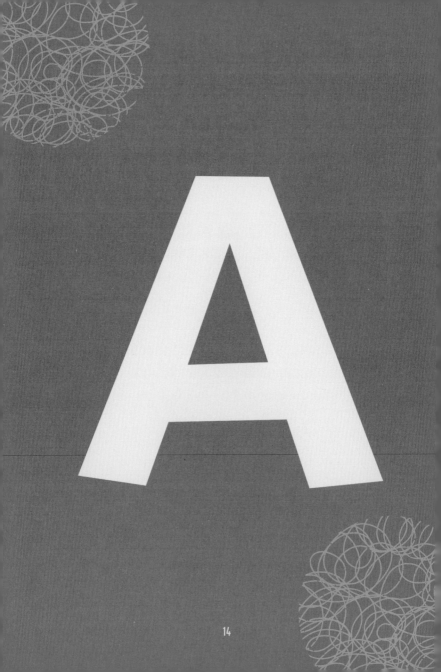

Abba

Abba, also spelled Aba, means father in Hebrew and most Semitic languages. It's believed to be a term of endearment used by Jesus while praying to God in the Old Testament. Abba is also a common address for fathers in Muslim families and could be a sweet name for any grandfather who has taken on a more fatherly or prominent masculine role.

There's an option for grandmothers here too; the famous actress Debbie Reynolds was referred to as Aba Daba by her grandchildren. Reynolds was the mother of actress Carrie Fisher (*Star Wars, When Harry Met Sally...*). Aba Daba is rhythmic and plays off baby babble, delightful for parents and young ones alike.

Amá sání,
Acheii & Análí

Amá sání (pronounced ah-ma sun-AYE) is Navajo for maternal grandmother. Acheii means maternal grandfather, and Análí means paternal grandmother or grandfather. Unless you are Navajo yourself, I would recommend that you avoid referring to yourself by these terms out of respect to Native Americans who hold their language sacred, especially after facing the risk of lingual extinction due to colonization. However, knowing more about other cultures' traditions is always beneficial to our understanding of the world and our place in it.

Amá sání means mother's mother and also refers to any of her sisters—so great-aunts as well. It's common in Native cultures to refer to elders as aunts or uncles even if they are not blood related because it's considered an honorific (formal name), recognizing their years of experience and place of wisdom in their family, community, and society.

Amma & Afi

The Icelandic names Amma and Afi sound like mama and poppy when spoken aloud. They mean grandmother and grandfather, respectively. It's worth mentioning that Amma also means mother in several other languages, like South Indian and Persian. Amma means "sweet, forgiving woman" in Icelandic. Afi (pronounced AH-vi) most likely comes from the Old Norse Viking word avus, meaning ancestor, which is usually masculine. Unlike other Scandinavian languages such as Norwegian, Swedish, Danish, and Faroese, Icelandic has changed very little since its linguistic beginnings.

Abuela & Abuelo

"My grandparents are Abuela and Abuelo, and I can't imagine calling them anything else.... They've lived close by my whole life, and I wouldn't want it any other way. I have friends with grandparents who live far away, and I feel bad for them because to me it's just the perfect way to learn from them and have more love in your life. They're different than my parents but also the same. They care so deeply about me and what I need to feel loved or succeed. I think it really helped my parents when I was a kid too because they could go straight to the source for help. It makes me excited to have kids and have several generations looking out for me and my family as it grows."

—Yessica, 22

Baba

A reference to the matriarch of the family, Baba is a Slavic word for grandmother that carries a weight and wisdom worthy of the woman in your family who made it all possible. Most popular in Eastern Europe, Baba is not only easy for your little one to pronounce, but also pays homage to the strong mothers in your family.

In Persian culture, however, Baba also means grandfather, as well as father, sir, and wise old man. It's an honorific for older men in the family, indicating the same earned respect as the name's feminine counterpart. Also used in several West Asian and South Asian cultures, Baba is no doubt an admirable name for the granddad-to-be.

Babushka

Another powerful grandmother title, Babushka is a name for Russian grandmothers who are soft-spoken and ferocious in the love they have to offer. This word often makes us imagine an a face worn with time and a headscarf that could be considered comical, but the word should be taken seriously, given the culture and care behind it. If the grandma-to-be comes from the old country or a more traditional background, Babushka may be worth trying out as a grandparent name. It all has to do with personality, preferences, and, of course, what the future grandkiddo wants too.

Big Daddy & Big Momma

For grandparents with big personalities, there's no better option than Big Daddy and Big Momma. Big Daddy and Big Momma are more common among Southern United States communities, but these are certainly nationwide namesakes for any grandparents who are worth their sauce and know it. This is a great option for grandparents who know their minds, speak up, and have lots of love to give. Also, just imagine a little kid walking up and saying, "Hi Big Daddy! Hi Big Momma!" That's an opportunity for comedic gold.

Bubba

Bubba is a sweet alternative to Grandpa. It suggests a gentle way of being—an immediate familiarity with your grandchildren that they will treasure for a lifetime. Whether it's the name being called to take the kids out for ice cream or the one your older grandchildren think of when they need to call someone they can count on, Bubba encapsulates the same honor as Grandpa does, but in a more modern way. One famous example of this is Michael Douglas, whose grandchildren call him Bubba.

Bubbe

Bubbe, pronounced "Bubbeh" or "Bubbee," is Yiddish for Grandma. There are a variety of spellings, including Bubby and Bubbie. Bubbe is what the late Justice Ruth Bader Ginsburg's grandchildren called her. Justice Bader Ginsburg was quoted in *The New Yorker* on March 11, 2013, saying, "It bothers me when people say to make it to the top of the tree you have to give up a family." The Notorious RBG is a fantastic example of a powerful grandmother; she cared deeply for her family, as well as families all over the United States during her 27 years on the Supreme Court.

CeeCee

For the grandma with a sweet "C" name, an equally lovely grandma name—like CeeCee—is an endearing option. This name only adds to the level of excitement as your grandbaby comes running to greet you at the door, shrieking, "CeeCee!" This name could also be spelled CeCe, Cici, or however suits your "fan-cee." If your name is Cecilia, Catherine, or anything with an opportunity for a "C" nickname, you've found the perfect one.

Coco

The honorific Coco is from the adored Disney/ Pixar 2017 hit film of the same name. Coco, the matriarch of the Rivera family, is protagonist Miguel's great-grandmother. She's sweet and kind, allowing Miguel to express himself in a way he can't around his parents or grandmother. Coco shares Miguel's love of music, which is forbidden in the Rivera household. And the ending is a real tear-jerker. If you haven't seen it yet, I highly recommend it. After you've finished watching, consider making Coco the name you'd like your grandkids to call you, and create a family legacy just like the Riveras in the film.

Cookie

This one is for the grandmother or grandfather who is always sweet. Cookie is a perfect name for grandparents who love to bake or share sweets, or who simply connect with this honorific alternative. Cookie is usually a name for grandmothers in the Southern United States, but it could be fitting for a grandpa too. Whether this grandparent loves to cook or is just a little kooky, Cookie is a great option that's lighthearted, simple, and wholesome. It's classic and cute, so keep it in mind as you think about your official grandparent title.

The Countess

Hear me out: The Countess is a fantastic name idea for the most elegant of grandmamas. All poise and polish, this is a perfect name for a fabulous grandmother who knows exactly what she's about. Opinionated and strong-willed, she's earned this title through years of experience raising a family. This is an ode to Dame Maggie Smith's beloved character in *Downton Abbey*: the Dowager Countess of Grantham. Known for her incredible one-liners, stubborn dedication to tradition (to an admirable extent!), and exquisite gowns and hats, she embodies everything that the name The Countess represents.

Dadi & Dada

Dadi and Dada refer to paternal grandparents in Hindi. Dadi means grandmother and Dada means grandfather. Maternal grandparents are called Nani and Nana—Nani refers to grandmother and Nana refers to grandfather. To indicate additional respect, you would refer to elders as Dadiji and Dadaji, and Naniji and Nanaji. Honorifics like this show appreciation and familial love among children and their grandparents. Consider whether you would like a more formal or casual grandparent name—or something that lies on the border between the two.

Daideó

Daideó, pronounced "dadj-yoh," means granddad in the Irish Gaelic language. The Irish word for grandfather is Seanáthair, which literally translates to "old father." It's more likely, though, that kids in Gaelic-speaking cultures would call their grandfather Daideó. This is paired with Mhamó (see page 72) and Seanmháthair, which mean grandmother and "wise mother" in Gaelic. Most kids in Ireland use Granddad or Granny to refer to their grandparents, but any families with Irish roots, those who speak Gaelic, or parents and grandparents who want to encourage an interest in Irish culture could try Daideó.

Dedushka

In Russian, you say Dedushka to refer to a grandfather. Paired with Babushka, which means grandmother (see page 21), you will be Dedushka i Babushka, meaning grandparents. Just like Babushka, Dedushka is used to refer to one's grandfather or to any elderly gentleman as a sign of respect. Dedushka isn't considered a formal title, but it's not impolite either. Dedushka is sometimes shortened to Deda. Finding variations of these culturally rooted names can help you determine the perfect fit for your grandparents' name pairing or individual name.

Deedle

"My granddad is called Deedle among members of my immediate family. He called me and my sister Littles, and one day one of us started to call him Deedle. I wish I could take credit, but I can't remember. It didn't—or doesn't—make a lot of sense when I say, 'My Deedle is coming to visit!' I remember a kid in elementary school made fun of me for calling my grandpa Deedle. So I stopped for a bit, but I remember he asked me one day to call him Deedle again. Because it was special to him and special to our family. He'll always be Deedle to me."

—Erick, 35

Eeya

My uncle Walter—my mom's oldest brother—was the first to become a grandpa among her nine siblings. Originally, I think my cousins tried to encourage their kiddos to call him G-Wa, short for Grandpa Walter, since it's cute, easy, and fun to say ("G-WAAAA!"). But he didn't want to be Grandpa, so one of the children came up with Eeya. Uncle Walter is an artist, so he created a whole path in his backyard called Eeya's Trail for the little ones to enjoy. It's full of sunflowers painted on the fence, rocks in the shape of mushrooms (which my uncle made himself), and a space for my little cousins to explore their creativity and adventurous sides.

Effie

"My grandmother was called Effie, since her real name was Elizabeth. It was a nickname her mother called her and that she wanted to be called by her grandchildren because it carried on her mom's memory. My name's not Elizabeth, so calling myself Effie would be random maybe, but I would kind of want to go by Effie when I have kids and grandkids, to keep it in our family. My Effie passed away years ago, but I still think of her every day."

—Haley, 28

F

Fafa

Fafa refers to your father's mother in Danish. Denmark is one of the happiest countries in the world. Hygge is a Danish term that literally translates to "the light of the soul." Hygge means creating cozy social gatherings and intimate get-togethers with family and friends. Create a hygge of your own or connect with your Danish roots with the name Fafa, and celebrate with everyone in your family who wants to welcome new life into your home.

Farmor & Farfar

Farmor and Farfar mean grandmother and grand-father, respectively, on your father's side. These names are widely used throughout Sweden and anywhere Swedish is commonly spoken. Distinguishing between paternal and maternal grandparents establishes family relations—and helps avoid arguing over who gets what name. Swedes extend this naming system to refer to their great-grandparents, great-great-grandparents, and more distant ancestors. Mormor (see page 74) means mother's mother/maternal grandmother in Swedish. Farmor and Farfar originate from Northern Sámi, the indigenous culture in Norway. Fun fact: the Northuldra tribe in Disney's *Frozen 2* is based on the Sámi.

Foxy

This name is perfect for the extremely stylish grandma who knows she's too young at heart to go by Grandma—no offense to the Grandmas out there! I love the thought of a grandma greeting her grandkids' friends by saying, "Call me Foxy!" I'm picturing lots of royal purple, glamorous makeup, and a little bit of attitude that only this type of grandma could pull off in a casual setting, because every event is formal when she's there. Consider adding Foxy to your list if it calls to you!

Gaia

Gaia, the Greek goddess of Earth, mother of all, epitomizes the beginning of life, power, and beauty. She is the reason that the mountains, seas, plains, rivers, and starry heavens were formed in Greek mythology. Newscaster Gayle King said she was "trying on anything" and considered Gaia after her grandson was born. "I don't want to be called Grandma or Nana," she said in a 2021 interview with *Entertainment Tonight*. "No offense to the Grandmas or Nanas! But I'm looking for a nice, fun grandma name. Right now, I kind of like Gaia because it means Mother Earth and it sounds like Gayle. But I don't know, I'm open. Maybe the baby will make up something!"

Gee/Gigi

My great-grandmother on my dad's side was named Helen, but we called her Gee (pronounced guh-EE). She lived to be 100 years old and crocheted more afghan blankets than you could ever imagine. My baby blanket (that I still adore to this day) is even named Gee-gee after her. My dad and his siblings talk about her sense of humor often, which they definitely got from her, and which my dad passed on to me and my sisters.

Gia Gia

Gia Gia (pronounced ya-ya) is how you say grandma in Greek. Also sometimes spelled YaYa or YiaYia, the name Gia Gia immediately invites feelings of comfort and love—and the promise of good food, which is roughly the same thing as far as I'm concerned. In ancient Greek, Yaya meant woman. Lena "Lenny" Kaligaris's grandmother from *Sisterhood of the Traveling Pants* (2005) is called Gia Gia. Especially when paired with Papou (see page 87), Gia Gia is a fun name for grandmothers, whether you have Grecian roots or just want something different from Grandma.

Glam-ma

Actress Goldie Hawn coined this fabulous phrase as a result of her own reluctance to go by Grandma. In Hawn's memoir (written together with author Wendy Holden), *Goldie: A Lotus Grows in the Mud* (2005, Berkley Trade), Hawn writes: "The wonderful day arrived; my grandson, Ryder Russell, burst forth into this world. I could barely contain myself. But was I really a 'grandmother'?" It is, Ms. Hawn continued, a "word that had so many connotations of old age and decrepitude." In a 2011 interview with *The New York Times,* Hawn said, "My son Oliver decided I should be called 'Glam-ma,' which I thought was quite brilliant and made us all laugh so hard." So Glam-ma it was!

Grandma/Gram/ Granny & Grandpa/ Gramp/Granddad

Would it really be *The A to Z of Grandparent Names* if I left out the classics? The names we all know and love? Grandma, Gram, Granny. Grandpa, Gramp, Granddad. These names really don't need an explanation. They're more than just names. They're a testament to the wise, caring, and supportive people in our lives who give love a new meaning. You may look for alternatives, but these grandparent names still have a special place in our hearts because of what they *really* mean. So here's to all the grannies, granddads, and more who take care of us.

Grump/ Grumpy

"My son couldn't say Gramp, so it came out as Grump. Which my parents tried not to find funny at first, but they did because my dad can be pretty grumpy. He softened up with our kids, but it took some time. You know, playing pretend and him muttering it wasn't real and not to be silly. You see him smiling, though, and know he's not so grouchy. I think they initially tried not to let Grump stick because of the connotations. It makes my dad sound mean and crotchety, but he warmed up. It became a bit of a joke in my family. Grump and Grumpy!"

—Tanner, 38

Halmoni & Halabeoji

In Korean, the words for, grandma and grandpa are Halmeoni (hal-mo-nee) and Halabeoji (hal-ah-bo-jee), respectively. Hal means grand, abeoji means father, and meoni means mother. Keep in mind that Halmeoni does not refer to a woman's age and would not be used casually like you might refer to women not related to you. These terms are transliterated, since the Korean language uses Hangul, a different alphabet from English. For that reason, it is sometimes spelled differently. For instance, Halmoni is the more common spelling, but it can also be spelled as Halmeoni or shortened to Halmi.

Happy

"I called my grandpa Happy because I couldn't say Pappy, which is what he wanted to be called. I think it's a cute name for anyone, but especially for him. He's so joyful and wholesome—he liked to dress up as Santa Claus when my siblings and I were little. I'm sure he'd do it again for my kids, if he's feeling up for it. It's different—and I think funny when you read my husband, Tanner's, [story] about how our kids call his dad Grump (see page 48). Sometimes we joke it's like *Snow White and the Seven Dwarfs* in our family: Grumpy, Happy. Maybe Granny and Mimi need new names."

—Hannah, 37

Honey

Another sweet and simple name, Honey is a lovely alternative to Grandma. Actress Susan Sarandon borrowed the name from a friend who used it for his grandmother. Honey encapsulates the warmth of grandmothers who want to host teatime in the garden and always have something kind to say. I imagine that a grandma who goes by Honey has a big smile and a deep understanding of what it means to love her family.

Iggy

Iggy stems from a nickname for Ignacio, Ignatius, and even Sigmund. It's a modern twist on an old-fashioned name, which is a fun way to think about any name you'd like to go by. If you're a grandparent looking for something different, think of the unique ways you can put a spin on traditional grandparent names, like Iggy (e.g., Ziggy, Jiggy). Maybe that inspires you to come up with a variation of your own name—the choice is up to you!

Jaryi

The Guaraní people are a powerful Indigenous tribe in Brazil. When I was in college, my social sciences professor worked directly with the Guaraní tribe to preserve their culture. They called her Jaguarete—Jaguar. It's common for the jaguar to be part of the beginning and end of a person's life in Guaraní culture. Perhaps this is why it sounds so much like Jaryi, the Guaraní word for grandmother. In more modern slang, Jaryi can mean spectacular or exceptional—just like grandmothers are!

Jefe

Jefe (heh-fay) means "boss" in Spanish. Former president George W. Bush's grandchildren call him Jefe. Initially, he wanted his grandchildren to call him Sir, but Jefe, which could also mean chief, found its way into the family order of state instead. (Keep in mind that it may be considered inappropriate to use this term if you're not a Spanish speaker yourself.) Late president George H. W. Bush went by Poppy, and late First Lady Barbara Bush's nickname was The Enforcer. And former First Lady Laura Bush revealed that she isn't Nana or Grandmother, but Mimi Maxwell—a name her daughters, Jenna and Barbara, made up for her.

Jidi

In the Lebanese dialect of Arabic, you would refer to a grandfather as Jid, and my grandfather as Jidi (pronounced zhid-dee). Jido means his grandfather. In other Arabic dialects, there are many ways to refer to one's grandparents, depending on the region and family preference. Sitty (grandmother) and Jeddou (grandfather) are common, but you may also hear Jiddee or Seedu for grandfather and Teta or Situ for grandmother.

KiKi

"We call my grandmother Kiki for a couple reasons. Her first name is Katherine, but when my parents offered that we could call her Gramma Kate, she stuck out her tongue and made a disgusted noise, so that was out. Then they thought maybe Gramma Kat, but she didn't like cats much and that was a hang-up. I was born, started baby babbling, and called out 'kikikiki' like a frog or some weird, small animal. Somehow, Kiki stuck. She loves the rhythm of it and likes to introduce herself to my friends as 'Kiki, that's me!' It suits her."

—Anonymous

Kuku Kane

Kuku Kane is the formal term for grandfather in Hawaiian. Kane (pronounced KA-nay) means man. Kane refers to one of the most powerful Hawaiian gods, the creator who gave life to the sun and sky. In early creation myths, Kane made man in his image from clay that originated in each of the four cardinal directions. He is considered the creative parent of man and all other living creatures. More commonly used in place of Kuku is the name Tutu, which means grandparent and can be used for all genders. There is technically no "t" in the Hawaiian language, so "t" and "k" are somewhat interchangeable.

Kuku Wahine

Kuku Wahine is the formal word for grandmother in Hawaiian. Wahine (pronounced wa-HEE-neigh) means woman. Just like Kuku/Tutu Kane (see page 61), Kuku Wahine can be informalized to Tutu and represents all genders. Noting the significance of gender-inclusive terms is important because, in Hawaiian culture, there is a third gender: Māhū. Māhū ("in the middle") are people with traditional and important social and spiritual roles. Tutu is also a unique name for grandparents and elders who are gender fluid or agender.

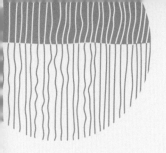

LaLa

LaLa, like Kiki (see page 60), can be the result of baby babble, and is a unique name that comes naturally to children. Lala could be a great name for grandmothers or grandfathers. LaLa is not a common name for grandparents, but it is fun and easy for little ones to pronounce. Whether your name is Lawson, Lane, or something else altogether, LaLa could be your new favorite nickname as a grandparent.

Lǎolao & Lǎoye

In the Northern Mandarin dialect, Lǎolao and Lǎoye mean grandmother and grandfather, respectively, in reference to maternal grandparents. Lǎo (pronounced la-OW) literally means female, referring to the maternal side of the family. Lǎolao and Lǎoye translate literally to female grandmother and female grandfather—again, to mean 'maternal,' indicating maternal grandparents. In the Southern dialect, maternal grandparents are called Wàipó and Wàigōng (see page 112). The rhythm of these names is lilting and lovely, resulting in an alluring alliteration that makes for a perfect pair of grandparent names.

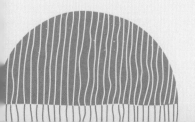

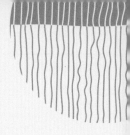

Lolly/Lolli & Pop

For expecting grandparents with a sense of humor, Lolly (or Lolli) and Pop are fun options. Playing off the familiar sweet we all know and love, it's a change from the traditional Grandma and Grandpa, while Pop still retains some of the same sound (without being too obvious). Grandmother can also go by Pop if she prefers! Either way, Lolly and Pop go together hand in hand, and are fun names for your inevitably sugar-loving grandchild.

Lovey

The most famous grandmother who goes by Lovey is none other than *Keeping Up with the Kardashians'* Kris Jenner. After deciding she didn't want to be called Grandma because Jenner found the traditional name didn't fit her, she landed on Lovey. Jenner has 10 grandchildren (so far!), and she's often seen wearing a necklace with "Lovey" engraved on it. It's a cute name, capturing the literal love you and your family have for one another, and we're sure Kris Jenner won't mind sharing.

Maman

Common among French-speaking populations, Maman is a variation of mother and a notable option for grandmothers who want to exude class, style, and wisdom. Other common names for grandmothers in French include Grand-maman, Grand-mére, and Mémère. Mémé and Mamie are usually used by French Canadians in Quebec. Connect with your French roots or your love of the language and discover a unique name for yourself with Maman.

Marmee

Marmee is the affectionate name that the March girls in *Little Women* use for their mother, Mrs. March. "Just call me Mother. Or Marmee, everyone does!" Marmee is likely a spin-off from Mommy or Mummy, with an added Boston accent. It's a wonderful idea for literary lovers and a nod to the power of feminine relationships as portrayed in Louisa May Alcott's most famous novel. You could also consider other variations and words for mothers and grandmothers from literature to find your perfect alternative to the traditional Grandmother. Just think how wonderful it will be to share your love of stories with your grandchildren!

Meemaw

This is a classic title for grandmothers with Southern roots, to be sure. One famous example of the use of Meemaw is in the TV show *The Big Bang Theory*, which ran for twelve seasons on CBS. Sheldon Cooper, genius and pop-culture icon, has a grandmother he loves and adores. Sheldon often refers to Meemaw throughout the series, describing her as wonderful, warm, loving, and sweet. Sheldon says that Meemaw calls him Moonpie because he is "nummy-nummy and she could just eat me up."

Mhamó

In Ireland, the traditional Gaelic term for grandmother is Mhamó (pronounced MA-mo), which is straightforward and easy enough to remember. Considerably more Gaelic are Maimeó (pronounced MA-mo) and Daideó (pronounced dadj-YO), Irish words for grandmother and grandfather, and Máthair Chríona (pronounced ma-HAIR cree-NAH), which translates to "wise mother" (and is a more formal term). All in all, Irish children are much more likely to use Maimeó or Móraí, or, more colloquially, Granny or Nana. If you want a unique way to connect your grandchildren with their Irish roots, Mhamó or one of the many other Irish honorifics listed here may be the name for you.

Mimi

Texas (in true Lone Star fashion) is the lone holdout for the name Mimi; in this state, that is the most popular grandmother name. Mimi is a charming Grandma alternative that's easy for young children to sound out. It expresses the sweetness and love that grandmothers are truly made to share. Ideal for anyone with an "M" name or a desire to find something different for the new little ones in their life to call them, you can't go wrong with Mimi.

Mormor

"My family is from Sweden, and my parents got pregnant with me in the '90s. I was the first grandbaby, so picking a name for their parents was a big deal. At that point, my grandparents had lived in the States a long time, and my mom was born here, so my grandmother was just going to be Grandma because it was easier. But when my grandma would come over to visit and help my mom, I would reach for her and say, 'More, more! Mormor!' It means 'mother's mother' in Swedish. It was fitting and it stuck, and I'm glad it did. My cousins call her something else, but to me she's Mormor."

—Maggie, 26

Bonus info:

Morfar means maternal grandfather in Swedish.

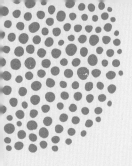

Nai Nai

Nai Nai denotes the father's mother (paternal grandmother) in the Southern Mandarin dialect. It translates to "respectfully, mistress of the house." There is a heavy emphasis on paying respect to the man's family in Chinese culture, so providing his mother with a strong title is important. It's also a formal way to address an older woman, indicating her wisdom and the respect she has earned. Nai Nai is accompanied by the name Yeye, which means paternal grandfather in Mandarin (see page 118).

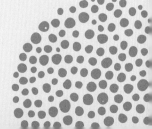

Nana/Nan/Nanny

My maternal grandmother was Nana, and it's the term my mother covets if/when my husband and I have our own kids. My grandmother's name was Nana Gert—short for Gertrude—and she was one of seven children born to Irish immigrants in New York. I recently traveled to Ireland, and it was lovely to hear locals call their grandmothers Nanny. Nan is also very common in the United Kingdom. I (and many others) have a soft spot in my heart for the simple and sweet name Nana.

Nonna & Nonno

In Italy, most grandmas and grandpas are respectfully called Nonna and Nonno. Many Italian Americans also use these names or another variation, Nonni, to pay tribute to their roots (also see Nonie on page 79). Nonnas are known for their culinary skills and passing the art of cooking down to members of their families to avoid losing recipes—and their legacy—to time. Grandparents are significant members of Italian culture. As the matriarchs and patriarchs of their families, they represent love and life lived fully.

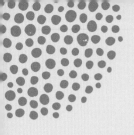

Nonie

Beloved children's author Judy Blume goes by
Nonie, a name as special as she is (and her books
are!). Blume has one grandchild, whom she credits
as the inspiration behind the most recent books
in her Fudge series. She has spoken about how she
loved reading to him as a child. She loves thinking
about how she passed on her love of books to her
children and then to her grandson. Maybe this
name will help remind you to pass on the things
you love!

Obaasan & Ojiisan

In Japanese, grandma and grandpa are formally referred to as Obaasan (pronounced oh-BAH-sahn) and Ojiisan (pronounced oh-JEE-sahn). Children are more likely to call their grandmothers the informal Sobo (see page 99), however, and their grandfathers Jiji (a derivative of the word for grandfather, Ojiisan). Baba is another variation for grandmothers. These names are a two-in-one deal: a formal name and nickname, so your grandchildren have a way to express their admiration and respect, and also a way to voice their love and affection.

Oma

"Oma is Dutch and German for grandmother. My parents moved to the Netherlands when my older sister was just born, so my Oma decided she wanted to be called that instead of Grandma. I was born there two and a half years later, and the rest is history!"

—Saskia, 25

Oopi

Whoopi Goldberg's great-granddaughter calls the famous comedian and *The View* host Oopi, while Goldberg's three grandchildren simply call her Granny. Recognizing that you may need more than one name as your family grows isn't a bad idea—not to mention that it's an opportunity to find more fun and special names!

Opa

German for grandfather, Opa is a gentle name for any expecting grandpa who wants to be called something different. Opa is informal, with Grossvater or Grossvader being the more formal terms in German—not to be confused with Darth Vader (who may not have been the best grandfather). Vader means father, and might have been a giveaway in the beloved *Star Wars* saga's most famous twist. Opa, on the other hand, carries no fictional-world baggage; it's the perfect name for a special grandparent.

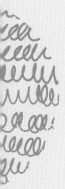

Papa/Pawpaw/ Pop-Pop

Papa is the most common nickname for grandfathers in 36 states. Those in Pennsylvania, New Jersey, Maryland, and Delaware tend to go for Pop or Pop-Pop. Southerners are more likely to use Papaw or Pawpaw. Papaw is the most common name for grandpa in Alabama, West Virginia, Louisiana, and Mississippi. Pawpaw is most popular in Arkansas, Indiana, Kentucky, and Tennessee. No matter your roots, this name could be a great option for you!

Pappous/Papou

Pappous and Papou are two great names that both mean grandpa in Greek. Tom Hanks is one famous name who also happens to go by Papou for a select few. You may also see Pappoo or Papu used as variations of this name; another, more affectionate term is Papouli. These are the American phonetic spellings, though—the Greek is actually παππούς. This name is perfectly paired with Gia Gia (see page 45).

Peach

In a March 2009 *People* article, Martin Sheen talked about his sons, Charlie Sheen and Emilio Estevez, his grandchildren, and what they call him. "From the time they were very small, they've referred to me as 'Peach,'" Martin Sheen explained. "I was always quoting Shakespeare, using highfalutin language when they were young. So they used to call me 'Grandpeachual.' And even now, they'll call me up and say, 'Hi Peach! How ya doin?'" Martin Sheen famously played President Bartlet in the Aaron Sorkin series *West Wing*, and recently concluded his role as Robert in the Netflix series *Grace and Frankie* (a hilarious show, great for grandparents who love a bit of dirty humor and quick wit!).

Pépère

Pépère (pronounced peh-PEAR) is a common moniker for grandfathers in French-speaking countries, especially Canada and France. It is best paired with Mémère, which is the common name for grandmother (see page 69). Grand-père is the formal term, while Pépère is more sarcastic, if anything, like "What are you doing, old man?" In Canada you may also see it spelled Pépé. Pépé can mean an old-timer who is quiet, calm, and thoughtful (as many grandfathers are). It encapsulates a feeling of gentle kindness and love.

Pip

When I taught at a summer music camp, one camper used this name to call to his grandfather at pickup time. The little boy would yell, "Pip!" at the top of his lungs and run through the auditorium into his grandpa's arms. Pip would swoop him up and give him a big squeeze before checking him out for the day, holding the boy's hand on one side and his lunchbox on the other. Maybe this name will hold the magic and excitement it did for that charming pair for you as well!

Queen/Queenie

In the same line of thought as The Countess (see page 29), Queen or Queenie is a fantastic name for a grandmother. Consider for a moment: Queen Clarisse of Genovia from *The Princess Diaries*, portrayed by the incomparable Dame Julie Andrews—an iconic grandma if there ever was one. This name will allow you to channel her grace and compassion. Queenie is another great option for the elegant grandma with a great sense of humor. You can choose between them or let your grandchild choose for you!

Royal

Royal, from the film *The Royal Tenenbaums*, is a sharpshooting businessman and the Tenenbaum patriarch. Royal (played by Gene Hackman) is set on proving to his family that he's changed. This classic Wes Anderson movie is full of stylish characters and tracksuits, and it features the redemptive tale of Royal, who reclaims his independence and sense of self at an older age. If you connect with his story, this name may be a great option for you!

Saba & Savta

Saba and Savta mean grandfather and grandmother, respectively, in Hebrew. Hebrew uses a different alphabet than English, making transliteration necessary. Words often come in several different spellings with the same meaning. For example, Savta can also be seen spelled as Safta, Savah, or Sabta.

Additionally, the word rabbi comes from the Hebrew word raba, meaning "great" or "revered." Saba is seen in the Hebrew expression saba raba (great-grandfather), and raba is also included in hatzlacha raba, meaning a blessing for much success. If you're Jewish, you might also consider the Yiddish names Zayde (see page 120) and Bubbe (see page 24).

Sassy

This could be a great name for the grandma or grandpa with the right attitude. This is a name you earn through quick wit, a smart remark that always earns a laugh, and an unwavering sense of self. If your grandchild proposed this name, I might understand some trepidation about it, but I think there's something admirable about owning your big personality! If that speaks to you, Sassy might be your perfect alternative grandparent name.

Shazza

Shazza is a departure from your typical grand-mother names. This fun name is donned by none other than *The Talk*'s former cohost Sharon Osbourne. One of daytime TV's most notable personalities, Sharon Osbourne doesn't like being called Grandma. Instead, her grandchildren all call her Missus O or Shazza, the British nickname for Sharon. Her husband, Ozzy, on the other hand, may go by "the Prince of Darkness" to Black Sabbath fans, but to their grandkids, Ozzy is simply Papa.

Sobo

Sobo is the informal term for grandmother in Japan. As mentioned, Obaasan and Ojiisan (see page 81) are the formal titles, and there's something to be said about a family name that your grandchildren use as a term of endearment rather than a formal name. An informal honorific still denotes respect and love, perhaps even more so because it's used solely among family members. The name you choose to represent your relationship with your grandchildren helps them understand the trust they should have in you and the love that binds you together.

Suga Mama

One of my favorite pop-culture grandmas is Suga Mama from *The Proud Family*. I grew up watching *The Proud Family* on Disney Channel: a delightful show with a fantastic opening theme by Destiny's Child (Beyoncé before she was Beyoncé?!), chaotic and wholesome family dynamics, and, thanks to Suga Mama, plenty of times I laughed out loud. Voiced by former *Family Matters* star Jo Marie Payton, Suga Mama is hilarious and untamable. Suga Mama fiercely defends her grandkids, especially Penny, the main character of the show. Suga Mama loves wrestling and her poodle, Puff. She's unapologetically herself and certainly worth a mention in this book. If you recognize yourself in her, maybe it's even worth borrowing her name to use as your grandparent honorific!

T

Tipuna

In the Māori Polynesian dialect, tipuna (pro-nounced ti-POO-nuh) sometimes refers to tribal elders. More commonly within the culture, though, tipuna means grandparents and ancestors. Male elders are also known as koroua (or koro for short), and female elders as kuia. They meet in a whare tupuna, ancestor house, to discuss tribal relations. You may have seen the movie *Whale Rider,* in which Kahu, the main character, is raised by her grandfather and tribe elder, Koro Apirana. Tipuna tāne is the term for male ancestor in the Eastern dialect—tupuna in the Western dialect. Tipuna or tupuna wahine refers to female ancestors.

Toots/Tootsie

This is a sweet name for a grandma who loves Tootsie Rolls or wants to have a little bit of a laugh when her grandkid says, "How's it goin', Toots?" It's a little bit old-fashioned, but you can revitalize it. It's perfect for any grandma who has a good sense of humor and is looking for a light and easy honorific. Chew on this option (just like a Tootsie Roll!) for your grandma names idea list.

Tutu Kane &
Tutu Wahine

These are the informal Hawaiian names for grandfather and grandmother. Flip back to "K" (specifically, page 61) to learn more about consonants in Hawaiian and why Tutu may be the perfect grandparent nickname for you!

Umakhulu

Umakhulu (pronounced u-MAK-oo-loo) means grandmother, the matriarch, in the African Xhosa dialect. Xhosa (pronounced know–suh) is one of the official languages of South Africa and Zimbabwe. It is a click language spoken as a first language by approximately 8.2 million people and as a second language by another 11 million in South Africa. The Roman alphabet is used for writing Xhosa, but Xhosa has several sounds that are not found in English. The clicks originated from the Khoisan (referring to the groups formerly known as the Hottentots and the Bushmen).

Una

Pronounced "Oona," the name Una has a beautiful history and deep lingual roots. With both Latin and Irish origins, Una means "one" and "only" in Latin and is also derived from the Irish word uan, meaning lamb. It also represents the Queen of the Fairies in Irish mythology. Overall, this "one and only" name is a great option for the matriarch of your family who is the personification of truth, beauty, and unity. There is no better name for a grandmother who gave life to a family and a legacy; that's truly magical.

Vivi

"We called my grandmother Vivi. I thought it was her name until I was 12 or something, only to find out it was Grace. I have older cousins who told me Vivi wasn't actually Vivi's name. It completely messed up my world for about 30 seconds, until they told me they called her that because she was saying 'Baby' to my cousin, her first grandkid, who couldn't pronounce it and called her 'Vivi' back. It's interesting to me how the names we give our grandparents have a way of picking themselves. It made it special because yeah, she was a grandma, but she's my Vivi."

—Crystal, 28

Vovó & Vovô

Vovó and Vovô are the Brazilian Portuguese terms for grandmother and grandfather. They're spelled (basically) the same but pronounced differently—"vo-vaw" and "vo-voh." Other common Portuguese names for grandmother and grandfather are Avó and Avô, which are the European Portuguese terms, as opposed to Brazilian Portuguese. Variations include Avozinha, Vovó, or just Vo. Both grandmothers and grandfathers are referred to as Avo, but again, the pronunciation is different. Avô, for a grandfather, is pronounced "a-voh," while Avó, for a grandmother, is pronounced "a-vaw."

Wàipó & Wàigōng

Wàipó and Wàigōng refer to maternal grand-
mother and grandfather, respectively, in the
Southern dialect of Mandarin. I came across these
terms while reading Emily X. R. Pan's debut novel,
The Astonishing Color of After. The main character,
Leigh, travels to Taiwan to find out more about her
mother, who passed away and turned into a bird.
Her grandparents, Waipo and Waigong, are key
characters. Her grandmother is also fondly called
Po-po by another character in the book. Wàipó and
Wàigōng do not refer linguistically to one side of
the family or another, as other Mandarin terms do.
They're more general, commonly used to refer to
someone's age and experience, denoting respect
for the individual using the honorific.

Woof

Emmy Award– and Tony Award–winner Blythe Danner's grandmother name was Lalo. But before Lalo stuck, Danner wanted to go by Woof. "My mom's hot and she didn't want to be called Grandma," Danner's daughter, Gwyneth Paltrow, said in an interview on the talk show *Chelsea Lately*. "So she kept trying to make the Woof thing stick. It's even her email address." If you're a dog-person kind of grandparent, Woof is a cute and simple alternative to more traditional names.

It's tricky finding grandparent name ideas that start with "X." If you come up with any, I admire your creativity!

Yaya

Whether you're going for the Greek Gia Gia (see page 45), meaning maternal grandmother, or love the phonetic spelling of Yaya, this is a fantastic grandma name. My immediate thought when I came across this name was the 2002 film *Divine Secrets of the Ya-Ya Sisterhood*, directed by Callie Khouri and starring Sandra Bullock, Ellen Burstyn, and Dame Maggie Smith. It follows a group of complicated and hilarious older women in the South; the Ya-Ya sisterhood is loyal, fierce, and an excellent example of grandmothers who are perfectly human.

Yeye

Yeye is Mandarin for paternal grandfather. It is also sometimes spelled as Yeh Yeh or Je Je. The formal term for paternal grandfather is Zufu. For maternal grandfathers, there is a difference between Northern China and Southern China (see Wàipó and Wàigōng on page 112). In the North, the most common term is Lǎoye (see page 65). Ye Ye sounds a bit like Mimi, which in the United States doesn't have documented linguistic roots. When choosing your name, remember that you can always go for something more culturally oriented—or even choose your name based on the sound and feel of it alone!

Zayde

Pronounced "Zaydeh" or "Zaydee," Zayde is grand-father in Yiddish. As previously mentioned, Saba and Savta (see page 96) are the formal terms for grandfather and grandmother in Hebrew. But Zayde, the more familial Yiddish term, is paired with Bubbe (see page 24), which means grand-mother. Zayde specifically means your own grand-father, but can also mean old man. If you decide to use Zayde and Bubbe, we fully expect bubbeleh ("sweetie" in Yiddish) to be in your lexicon.

ZeeZee

Catherine Zeta-Jones's step-grandchildren call her Zee-Zee, no doubt because of her first last name, Zeta. Zeta-Jones is married to Michael Douglas, whose grandchildren call him Bubba (see page 23). Zeta-Jones is well-known for her roles in *The Mask of Zorro* (1998), *Entrapment* (1999), and *Chicago* (2002). She's glamorous and a wonderful example of a step-grandmother who has so much love to give. Her step-granddaughter, Lua, was born to her stepson, Cameron, in 2017.

Zsa Zsa

Zsa Zsa (sja-sja) is the informal Polish word for grandmother. The formal terms are Babcia and Babka. Other informal terms include Jaja, Busha, Busia, and Gigi. Zsa Zsa is also a girl's name commonly used in Eastern Europe, meaning "God is my oath." Zsa Zsa is a Hungarian nickname, sometimes used independently of its grandmother meaning; for instance, it's been linked for decades with the Hungarian-born actress Zsa Zsa Gabor. She was crowned Miss Hungary in 1936 and emigrated from Hungary to the United States in 1941.

Zumu

Zumu is the formal term to refer to a paternal grandmother in Mandarin. In this language, the most commonly used name for a paternal grandmother is Nai Nai, which is also sometimes spelled Nie Nie. For maternal grandmothers, Lǎolao is commonly used (see page 65), with Zumu being the more formal term. Zu refers to ancestor. For other Mandarin terms, check out Wàipó and Wàigong (see page 112).

AUTHOR BIO

Katie Hankinson holds a master of fine arts in creative writing and editing from Regis University and a bachelor's degree in writing and cultural anthropology from Fort Lewis College. She has served as a journalist, photographer, copywriter, freelance author, and editor for nearly 10 years. Her creative work has appeared in *Images Literary Magazine*, and she is in the process of finishing her YA fiction novel about two sisters experiencing the ripple effect of mental illness. In her free time, Katie and her husband, Josh, love to explore the Denver-Boulder metro area and care for their two cats, Peanut and Mac.

About Cider Mill Press Book Publishers

Good ideas ripen with time. From seed to harvest, Cider Mill Press brings fine reading, information, and entertainment together between the covers of its creatively crafted books. Our Cider Mill bears fruit twice a year, publishing a new crop of titles each spring and fall.

CIDER MILL
PRESS

BOOK
PUBLISHERS

"Where Good Books Are Ready for Press"

501 Nelson Place
Nashville, TN 37214

cidermillpress.com